John Augustus Barron

The Bills of Exchange Act 1890

Fully and Copiously Indexed so as to be of Quick and Ready Reference

John Augustus Barron

The Bills of Exchange Act 1890
Fully and Copiously Indexed so as to be of Quick and Ready Reference

ISBN/EAN: 9783337112110

Printed in Europe, USA, Canada, Australia, Japan

Cover: Foto ©Suzi / pixelio.de

More available books at **www.hansebooks.com**

THE

BILLS OF EXCHANGE ACT 1890.

FULLY AND COPIOUSLY INDEXED
SO AS TO BE OF QUICK AND
READY REFERENCE.

BY

JOHN AUGUSTUS BARRON

(ONE OF HER MAJESTY'S COUNSEL)

AUTHOR OF

Barron on Bills of Sale and Chattel Mortgages, and of
The Conditional Sales Act (annotated).

TORONTO:
CARSWELL & CO., PUBLISHERS.

1890.

PRINTED BY
THOS. MOORE & CO., LAW PRINTERS
22 & 24 ADELAIDE ST. EAST
TORONTO.

PREFACE.

A PERUSAL and consideration of the Bills of Exchange Act, 1890, made necessary by the active practice of my profession, induced the belief that simply an Index to the Act, carefully and accurately prepared, would commend itself to those in my profession, or in business, having frequent occasion to refer to the law.

With a hope that my belief will be justified I present its result, which, if found useful, will be my reward.

J. A. B.

53 VICTORIA.

CHAPTER 33.

An Act relating to Bills of Exchange, Cheques, and Promissory Notes.

[Assented to 16th May, 1890.]

HER MAJESTY, by and with the advice and consent of the Senate and House of Commons of Canada, enacts as follows ;—

PART I.

PRELIMINARY.

1. This Act may be cited as "*The Bills of Exchange* Short title. *Act,* 1890."

2. In this Act, unless the context otherwise requires,— Interpretation.

(*a*) The expression " Acceptance " means an acceptance "Acceptance." completed by delivery or notification ;

(*b*) The expression " Action " includes counter claim and "Action." set off ;

(*c*) The expression "Bank " means an incorporated bank "Bank" or savings bank carrying on business in Canada ;

(*d*) The expression " Bearer " means the person in pos- "Bearer" session of a bill or note which is payable to bearer ;

"Bill;"
"Note."   (e) The expression " Bill " means bill of exchange, and " Note " means promissory note ;

"Delivery."   (f) The expression " Delivery " means transfer of possession, actual or constructive, from one person to another ;

"Holder."   (g) The expression " Holder " means the payee or indorsee of a bill or note who is in possession of it, or the bearer thereof ;

"Indorsement."   (h) The expression " Indorsement " means an indorsement completed by delivery ;

"Issue."   (i) The expression " Issue " means the first delivery of a bill or note, complete in form, to a person who takes it as a holder ;

"Value."   (j) The expression " Value " means valuable consideration.

"Defence."   (k) The expression " Defence " includes counter-claim.

PART II.

BILLS OF EXCHANGE.

Form and Interpretation.

3. A bill of exchange is an unconditional order in writing, addressed by one person to another, signed by the person giving it, requiring the person to whom it is addressed to pay, on demand or at a fixed or determinable future time, a sum certain in money to or to the order of a specified person, or to bearer : *Bill of exchange defined.*

2. An instrument which does not comply with these conditions, or which orders any act to be done in addition to the payment of money, is not, except as hereinafter provided, a bill of exchange : *When instrument is not such bill.*

3. An order to pay out of a particular fund is not unconditional within the meaning of this section ; but an unqualified order to pay, coupled with (*a*) an indication of a particular fund out of which the drawee is to re-imburse himself, or a particular account to be debited with the amount, or (*b*) a statement of the transaction which gives rise to the bill, is unconditional : *Unconditional order defined.*

4. A bill is not invalid by reason— *Bill not invalid for reasons specified.*

(*a*) That it is not dated ;

(*b*) That it does not specify the value given, or that any value has been given therefor ;

(*c*) That it does not specify the place where it is drawn or the place where it is payable.

Inland and foreign bills.

4. An inland bill is a bill which is, or on the face of it purports to be, (*a*) both drawn and payable within Canada, or (*b*) drawn within Canada upon some person resident therein. Any other bill is a foreign bill :

If not noted as foreign.

2. Unless the contrary appears on the face of the bill, the holder may treat it as an inland bill.

If different parties to bill are the same person.

5. A bill may be drawn payable to, or to the order of, the drawer ; or it may be drawn payable to, or to the order of, the drawee :

Option of holder in case specified.

2. Where in a bill drawer and drawee are the same person, or where the drawee is a fictitious person or a person not having capacity to contract, the holder may treat the instrument, at his option, either as a bill of exchange or as a promissory note.

Drawee to be named.

6. The drawee must be named or otherwise indicated in a bill with reasonable certainty :

If there are more than one.

2. A bill may be addressed to two or more drawees, whether they are partners or not ; but an order addressed to two drawees in the alternative, or to two or more drawees in succession is not a bill of exchange.

Certainty required as to payee.

7. Where a bill is not payable to bearer, the payee must be named or otherwise indicated therein with reasonable certainty :

If payable to two or more payees, or to holder of office.

2. A bill may be made payable to two or more payees jointly, or it may be made payable in the alternative to one of two, or one or some of several payees. A bill may also be made payable to the holder of an office for the time being :

If payee is non-existing.

3. Where the payee is a fictitious or non-existing person, the bill may be treated as payable to bearer.

8. When a bill contains words prohibiting transfer, or indicating an intention that it should not be transferable, it is valid as between the parties thereto, but it is not negotiable : *Certain bills valid but not negotiable.*

2. A negotiable bill may be payable either to order or to bearer : *Payable to order or bearer.*

3. A bill is payable to bearer which is expressed to be so payable, or on which the only or last indorsement is an indorsement in blank : *To bearer.*

4. A bill is payable to order which is expressed to be so payable, or which is expressed to be payable to a particular person, and does not contain words prohibiting transfer or indicating an intention that it should not be transferable : *To order.*

5. Where a bill, either originally or by indorsement, is expressed to be payable to the order of a specified person, and not to him or his order, it is nevertheless payable to him or his order, at his option. *Option of payee.*

9. The sum payable by a bill is a sum certain within the meaning of this Act, although it is required to be paid— *Sum payable.*

(*a*) With interest ;

(*b*) By stated instalments ;

(*c*) By stated instalments, with a provision that upon default in payment of any instalment the whole shall become due ;

(*d*) According to an indicated rate of exchange, or according to a rate of exchange to be ascertained as directed by the bill ;

Discrepancy between figures and words. 2. Where the sum payable is expressed in words and also in figures, and there is a discrepancy between the two, the sum denoted by the words is the amount payable:

Interest. 3. Where a bill is expressed to be payable with interest, unless the instrument otherwise provides, interest runs from the date of the bill, and if the bill is undated, from the issue thereof.

Bill payable on demand. 10. A bill is payable on demand—

(a) Which is expressed to be payable on demand, or on presentation; or

(b) In which no time for payment is expressed:

Acceptance, etc., when overdue. 2. Where a bill is accepted or indorsed when it is overdue, it shall, as regards the acceptor who so accepts, or any indorser who so indorses it, be deemed a bill payable on demand.

Bill payable at a future time. 11. A bill is payable at a determinable future time, within the meaning of this Act, which is expressed to be payable—

(a) At a fixed period after date or sight:

(b) On or at a fixed period after the occurrence of a specified event which is certain to happen, though the time of happening is uncertain:

As to contingencies. 2. An instrument expressed to be payable on a contingency is not a bill, and the happening of the event does not cure the defect.

Omission of date in bill payable after date. 12. Where a bill expressed to be payable at a fixed period after date is issued undated, or where the acceptance of a bill payable at a fixed period after sight is undated, any holder may insert therein the true date of issue or acceptance, and the bill shall be payable accordingly;

Provided that (*a*) where the holder in good faith and by *As to wrong date.* mistake inserts a wrong date, and (*b*) in every case where a wrong date is inserted, if the bill subsequently comes into the hands of a holder in due course, the bill shall not be voided thereby, but shall operate and be payable as if the date so inserted had been the true date.

13. Where a bill or an acceptance, or any indorsement *Date prima facie evidence.* on a bill, is dated, the date shall, unless the contrary is proved, be deemed to be the true date of the drawing, acceptance, or indorsement, as the case may be:

2. A bill is not invalid by reason only that it is antedated *Certain datings not to invalidate.* or postdated, or that it bears date on a Sunday or other non-juridical day.

14. Where a bill is not payable on demand, the day on *Computation of time of payment.* which it falls due is determined as follows:

(*a*) Three days, called days of grace, are, in every case *Days of grace.* where the bill itself does not otherwise provide, added to the time of payment as fixed by the bill, and the bill is due and payable on the last day of grace: Provided that—

(1.) Whenever the last day of grace falls on a legal holi- *Non-juridical days.* day or non-juridical day in the Province where any such bill is payable, then the day next following, not being a legal holiday or non-juridical day in such Province, shall be the last day of grace:

2. In all matters relating to bills of exchange the follow- *What shall be such.* ing and no other shall be observed as legal holidays or non-juridical days, that is to say:

In all Provinces except Quebec.   (*a*) In all the Provinces of Canada, except the Province of Quebec—

> Sundays ;
> New Year's Day :
> Good Friday :
> Easter Monday ;
> Christmas Day ;

The birthday (or the day fixed by proclamation for the celebration of the birthday) of the reigning Sovereign ; and if such birthday is a Sunday, then the following day ;

The first day of July (Dominion Day), and if that day is a Sunday, then the second day of July as the same holiday ;

Any day appointed by proclamation for a public holiday, or for a general fast, or a general thanksgiving throughout Canada ; and the day next following New Year's Day and Christmas Day, when those days respectively fall on Sunday ;

In Quebec.   (*b*) And in the Province of Quebec the said days, and also—

> The Epiphany ;
> The Annunciation ;
> The Ascension ;
> Corpus Christi ;
> St. Peter and St. Paul's Day ;
> All Saints' Day ;
> Conception Day ;

In every Province.   (*c*) And also, in any one of the Provinces of Canada, any day appointed by proclamation of the Lieutenant-Governor of such Province for a public holiday, or for a fast or thanksgiving within the same, or being a non-juridical day by virtue of a statute of such Province :

3. Where a bill is payable at sight, or at a fixed period *Days to be computed when time begins to run* after date, after sight, or after the happening of a specified event, the time of payment is determined by excluding the day from which the time is to begin to run and by including the day of payment :

4. Where a bill is payable at sight or a fixed period after *When time begins to run.* sight, the time begins to run from the date of the acceptance if the bill is accepted, and from the date of noting or protest if the bill is noted or protested for non-acceptance, or for non-delivery :

5. The term " Month " in a bill means the calendar *Months.* month :

6. Every bill which is made payable at a month or *Reckoning of time.* months after date becomes due on the same numbered day of the month in which it is made payable as the day on which it is dated—unless there is no such day in the month in which it is made payable, in which case it becomes due on the last day of that month—with the addition, in all cases, of the days of grace.

15. The drawer of a bill and any indorser may insert *Case of need.* therein the name of a person to whom the holder may resort in case of need, that is to say, in case the bill is dishonored by non-acceptance or non-payment. Such person is called the referee in case of need. It is in the option of the holder to resort to the referee in case of need or not, as he thinks fit.

16. The drawer of a bill, and any indorser, may insert *Optional stipulations by drawer or indorser.* therein an express stipulation—

(*a*) Negativing or limiting his own liability to the holder ;

(*b*) Waiving, as regards himself, some or all of the holder's duties.

Definition of acceptance.

17. The acceptance of a bill is the signification by the drawee of his assent to the order of the drawer :

Requisites of acceptance.

2. An acceptance is invalid, unless it complies with the following conditions, namely :—

(*a*) It must be written on the bill and be signed by the drawee. The mere signature of the drawee without additional words is sufficient ;

(*b*) It must not express that the drawee will perform his promise by any other means than the payment of money ;

3. Where in a bill the drawee is wrongly designated or his name is misspelt, he may accept the bill as therein described, adding, if he thinks fit, his proper signature, or he may accept by his proper signature.

Time for acceptance.

18. A bill may be accepted—

(*a*) Before it has been signed by the drawer, or while otherwise incomplete ;

(*b*) When it is overdue, or after it has been dishonored by a previous refusal to accept, or by non-payment :

Date, in case of acceptance after dishonor.

2. When a bill payable after sight is dishonored by non-acceptance, and the drawee subsequently accepts it, the holder, in the absence of any different agreement, is entitled to have the bill accepted as of the date of first presentment to the drawee for acceptance.

General and qualified acceptances.

19. An acceptance is either (*a*) general, or (*b*) qualified : a general acceptance assents without qualification to the order of the drawer ; a qualified acceptance in express terms varies the effect of the bill as drawn :

Qualified acceptance.

2. In particular, an acceptance is qualified which is—

(*a*) Conditional, that is to say, which makes payment by the acceptor dependent on the fulfilment of a condition therein stated ; but an acceptance to pay at a particular specified place is not conditional or qualified.

(*b*) Partial, that is to say, an acceptance to pay part only of the amount for which the bill is drawn ;

(*c*) Qualified as to time ;

(*d*) The acceptance of some one or more of the drawees, but not of all.

20. Where a simple signature on a blank paper is de- Inchoate instruments. livered by the signer in order that it may be converted into a bill, it operates as a *prima facie* authority to fill it up as a complete bill for any amount, using the signature for that of the drawer, or the acceptor, or an indorser : and, in like manner, when a bill is wanting in any material particular, the person in possession of it has a *prima facie* authority to fill up the omission in any way he thinks fit :

2. In order that any such instrument when completed When to be filled up. may be enforceable against any person who became a party thereto prior to its completion, it must be filled up within a reasonable time, and strictly in accordance with the authority given ; reasonable time for this purpose is a question of fact :

Provided, that if any such instrument, after completion, As to subsequent holder. is negotiated to a holder in due course, it shall be valid and effectual for all purposes in his hands, and he may enforce it as if it had been filled up within a reasonable time and strictly in accordance with the authority given.

21. Every contract on a bill, whether it is the drawer's, Contract not complete until delivery. the acceptor's or an indorser's, is incomplete and revocable, until delivery of the instrument in order to give effect thereto :

Exception.

Provided, that where an acceptance is written on a bill, and the drawee gives notice to, or according to the directions of, the person entitled to the bill that he has accepted it, the acceptance then becomes complete and irrevocable :

Requisites as to delivery.

2. As between immediate parties, and as regards a remote party, other than a holder in due course, the delivery—

(*a*) In order to be effectual must be made either by or under the authority of the party drawing, accepting or indorsing, as the case may be ;

(*b*) May be shown to have been conditional or for a special purpose only, and not for the purpose of transferring the property in the bill ;

When valid delivery presumed.

But if the bill is in the hands of a holder in due course, a valid delivery of the bill by all parties prior to him, so as to make them liable to him, is conclusively presumed :

Prima facie evidence.

3. Where a bill is no longer in the possession of a party who has signed it as drawer, acceptor or indorser, a valid and uncondititional delivery by him is presumed until the contrary is proved.

Capacity and Authority of Parties.

Capacity of parties.

22. Capacity to incur liability as a party to a bill is co-extensive with capacity to contract :

As to corporations.

Provided, that nothing in this section shall enable a corporation to make itself liable as drawer, acceptor or indorser of a bill, unless it is competent to it so to do under the law for the time being in force relating to such corporation :

Drawing or indorsing by person not competent.

2. Where a bill is drawn or indorsed by an infant, minor, or corporation having no capacity or power to incur liability on a bill, the drawing or indorsement entitles the

holder to receive payment of the bill, and to enforce it against any other party thereto.

23. No person is liable as drawer, indorser, or acceptor of a bill who has not signed it as such : Provided that— *Signature essential to liability.*

(*a*) Where a person signs a bill in a trade or assumed name, he is liable thereon as if he had signed it in his own name ; *Exceptions.*

(*b*) The signature of the name of a firm is equivalent to the signature by the person so signing of the names of all persons liable as partners in that firm.

24. Subject to the provisions of this Act, where a signature on a bill is forged or placed thereon without the authority of the person whose signature it purports to be, the forged or unauthorized signature is wholly inoperative, and no right to retain the bill or to give a discharge therefor or to enforce payment thereof against any party thereto can be acquired through or under that signature, unless the party against whom it is sought to retain or enforce payment of the bill is precluded from setting up the forgery or want of authority : *Forged or unauthorized signature.*

Provided, that nothing in this section shall affect the ratification of an unauthorized signature not amounting to a forgery : And provided also, that if a cheque, payable to order, is paid by the drawee upon a forged indorsement out of the funds of the drawer, or is so paid and charged to his account, the drawer shall have no right of action against the drawee for the recovery back of the amount so paid, or no defence to any claim made by the drawee for the amount so paid, as the case may be, unless he gives notice in writing of such forgery to the drawee within one year after he has acquired notice of such forgery ; and in case of *Proviso. Proviso as to payment on forged indorsement.*

failure by the drawer to give such notice within the said period, such cheque shall be held to have been paid in due course as respects every other party thereto or named therein, who has not previously instituted proceedings for the protection of his rights.

Procuration signatures. **25.** A signature by procuration operates as notice that the agent has but a limited authority to sign, and the principal is bound by such signature only if the agent in so signing was acting within the actual limits of his authority.

Person signing as agent or in representative capacity. **26.** Where a person signs a bill as drawer, indorser or acceptor, and adds words to his signature indicating that he signs for or on behalf of a principal, or in a representative character, he is not personally liable thereon ; but the mere addition to his signature of words describing him as an agent, or as filling a representative character, does not exempt him from personal liability :

Rule for determination of signature. 2. In determining whether a signature on a bill is that of the principal or that of the agent by whose hand it is written, the construction most favorable to the validity of the instrument shall be adopted.

The Consideration for a Bill.

Valuable consideration ; how constituted **27.** Valuable consideration for a bill may be constituted by—-

(*a*) Any consideration sufficient to support a simple contract ;

(*b*) An antecedent debt or liability ; such a debt or liability is deemed valuable consideration, whether the bill is payable on demand or at a future time :

When holder is holder for value. 2. Where value has at any time been given for a bill, the holder is deemed to be a holder for value as regards

the acceptor and all parties to the bill who became parties
prior to such time :

3. Where the holder of a bill has a lien on it, arising As to lien.
either from contract or by implication of law, he is deemed
to be a holder for value to the extent of the sum for which
he has a lien.

28. An accommodation party to a bill is a person who Accommodation
has signed a bill as drawer, acceptor, or indorser, without party to a
bill.
receiving value therefor, and for the purpose of lending his
name to some other person :

2. An accommodation party is liable on the bill to a His liability.
holder for value ; and it is immaterial whether, when such
holder took the bill, he knew such party to be an accomo-
dation party or not.

29. A holder in due course is a holder who has taken a Holder in
due course.
bill, complete and regular on the face of it, under the following conditions, namely :—

(a) That he became the holder of it before it was overdue and without notice that it had been previously dishonored, if such was the fact ;

(b) That he took the bill in good faith and for value,
and that at the time the bill was negotiated to him he had
no notice of any defect in the title of the person who
negotiated it :

2. In particular, the title of a person who negotiates a Title defective in
bill is defective within the meaning of this Act when he cases specified.
obtained the bill, or the acceptance thereof, by fraud,
duress, or force and fear, or other unlawful means, or for
an illegal consideration, or when he negotiates it in breach
of faith, or under such circumstances as amount to a
fraud :

Right of
subsequent
holder.

3. A holder, whether for value or not, who derives his title to a bill through a holder in due course, and who is not himself a party to any fraud or illegality affecting it, has all the rights of that holder in due course as regards the acceptor and all parties to the bill prior to that holder.

Presumption of value and good faith.

30. Every party whose signature appears on a bill is *prima facie* deemed to have become a party thereto for value :

On whom burden of proof lies.

2. And every holder of a bill is *prima facie* deemed to be a holder in due course ; but if, in an action on a bill, it is admitted or proved that the acceptance, issue or subsequent negotiation of the bill is affected with fraud, duress, or force and fear, or illegality, the burden of proof that he is such holder in due course shall be on him, unless and until he proves that, subsequent to the alleged fraud or illegality, value has in good faith been given for the bill by some other holder in due course :

Usurious consideration.

3. No bill, although given for a usurious consideration or upon a usurious contract, is void in the hands of a holder, unless such holder had at the time of its transfer to him, actual knowledge that it was originally given for a usurious consideration, or upon a usurious contract :

Consideration consisting of purchase money of patent right.

4. Every bill or note the consideration of which consists, in whole or in part, of the purchase money of a patent right, or of a partial interest, limited geographically or otherwise, in a patent right, shall have written or printed prominently and legibly across the face thereof, before the same is issued, the words "given for a patent right :" and without such words thereon such instrument and any renewal thereof shall be void, except in the hands of a holder in due course without notice of such consideration.

5. The indorsee or other transferee of any such instru- Liability of transferee. ment having the words aforesaid so printed or written thereon, shall take the same subject to any defence or set-off in respect of the whole or any part thereof which would have existed between the original parties :

6. Every one who issues, sells or transfers, by indorse- Penalty. ment or delivery, any such instrument not having the words "given for a patent right" printed or written in manner aforesaid across the face thereof, knowing the consideration of such instrument to have consisted, in whole or in part, of the purchase money of a patent right, or of a partial interest, limited geographically or otherwise, in a patent right, is guilty of a misdemeanor, and liable to imprisonment for any term not exceeding one year, or to such fine, not exceeding two hundred dollars, as the court thinks fit.

Negotiation of Bills.

31. A bill is negotiated when it is transferred from one Negotiation of bills. person to another in such a manner as to constitute the transferee the holder of the bill :

2. A bill payable to bearer is negotiated by delivery : To bearer.

3. A bill payable to order is negotiated by the indorse- To order. ment of the holder completed by delivery :

4. Where the holder of a bill payable to his order trans- Without indorsement. fers it for value without indorsing it, the transfer gives the transferee such title as the transferrer had in the bill, and the transferee in addition acquires the right to have the indorsement of the transferrer :

5. Where any person is under obligation to indorse a Personal liability may be avoided. bill in a representative capacity, he may indorse the bill in such terms as to negative personal liability.

B.E.A. 2

Requisites of a valid indorsement.

32. An indorsement in order to operate as a negotiation must comply with the following conditions, namely :—

(a) It must be written on the bill itself and be signed by the indorser. The simple signature of the indorser on the bill, without additional words, is sufficient ;

An indorsement written on an allonge, or on a " copy " of a bill issued or negotiated in a country where " copies " are recognized, is deemed to be written on the bill itself ;

(b) It must be an indorsement of the entire bill. A partial indorsement, that is to say, an indorsement which purports to transfer to the indorsee a part only of the amount payable, or which purports to transfer the bill to two or more indorsees severally, does not operate as a negotiation of the bill ;

(c) Where a bill is payable to the order of two or more payees or indorsees who are not partners, all must indorse, unless the one indorsing has authority to indorse for the others :

Misspelling

2. Where, in a bill payable to order, the payee or indorsee is wrongly designated, or his name is misspelt, he may indorse the bill as therein described, adding his proper signature ; or he may indorse by his own proper signature.

Order of indorsement.

3. Where there are two or more indorsements on a bill, each indorsement is deemed to have been made in the order in which it appears on the bill, until the contrary is proved :

Special indorsement.

4. An indorsement may be made in blank or special. It may also contain terms making it restrictive.

Conditional indorsement.

33. Where a bill purports to be indorsed conditionally, the condition may be disregarded by the payer, and payment to the indorsee is valid, whether the condition has been fulfilled or not.

34. An indorsement in blank specifies no indorsee, and a bill so indorsed becomes payable to bearer : *Indorsement in blank.*

2. A special indorsement specifies the person to whom, or to whose order, the bill is to be payable : *Special indorsement.*

3. The provisions of this Act relating to a payee apply, with the necessary modifications, to an indorsee under a special indorsement : *Application of Act to indorsee.*

4. Where a bill has been indorsed in blank, any holder may convert the blank indorsement into a special indorsement by writing above the indorser's signature a direction to pay the bill to or to the order of himself or some other person. *Conversion of blank indorsement.*

35. An indorsement is restrictive which prohibits the further negotiation of the bill, or which expresses that it is a mere authority to deal with the bill as thereby directed, and not a transfer of the ownership thereof, as, for example, if a bill is indorsed "Pay D only," or "Pay D for the account of X," or "Pay D, or order, for collection :" *Restrictive indorsement.*

2. A restrictive indorsement gives the indorsee the right to receive payment of the bill and to sue any party thereto that his indorser could have sued, but gives him no power to transfer his rights as indorsee unless it expressly authorizes him to do so : *Right of indorsee thereunder.*

3. Where a restrictive indorsement authorizes further transfer, all subsequent indorsees take the bill with the same rights and subject to the same liabilities as the first indorsee under the restrictive indorsement. *If further transfer is authorized.*

When negotiable bills ceases to be so. **36.** Where a bill is negotiable in its origin, it continues to be negotiable until it has been (*a*) restrictively indorsed, or (*b*) discharged by payment or otherwise :

Negotiation of overdue bill. 2. Where an overdue bill is negotiated, it can be negotiated only subject to any defect of title affecting it at its maturity, and thenceforward no person who takes it can acquire or give a better title than that which had the person from whom he took it :

When bill deemed overdue. 3. A bill payable on demand is deemed to be overdue within the meaning and for the purposes of this section, when it appears on the face of it to have been in circulation for an unreasonable length of time ; what is an unreasonable length of time for this purpose is a question of fact :

Presumption as to negotiation. 4. Except where an indorsement bears date after the maturity of the bill, every negotiation is *prima facie*, deemed to have been effected before the bill was overdue :

Taking bill subsequent to dishonor. 5. Where a bill which is not overdue has been dishonored, any person who takes it with notice of the dishonor takes it subject to any defect of title attaching thereto at the time of dishonor ; but nothing in this subsection shall affect the rights of a holder in due course.

Negotiation of bill to party already liable thereon. **37.** Where a bill is negotiated back to the drawer, or to a prior indorser, or to the acceptor, such party may, subject to the provisions of this Act, re-issue and further negotiate the bill, but he is not entitled to enforce the payment of the bill against any intervening party to whom he was previously liable.

Rights of the holder. **38.** The rights and powers of the holder of a bill are as follows :

(*a*) He may sue on the bill in his own name ;

(*b*) Where he is a holder in due course, he holds the bill free from any defect of title of prior parties, as well as from mere personal defences available to prior parties among themselves, and may enforce payment against all parties liable on the bill ;

(*c*) Where his title is defective, (1) if he negotiates the bill to a holder in due course, that holder obtains a good and complete title to the bill, and (2) if he obtains payment of the bill the person who pays him in due course gets a valid discharge for the bill.

General Duties of the Holder.

39. Where a bill is payable at sight or after sight, presentment for acceptance is necessary in order to fix the maturity of the instrument : *When presentment for acceptance is necessary.*

2. Where a bill expressly stipulates that it shall be presented for acceptance, or where a bill is drawn payable elsewhere than at the residence or place of business of the drawee, it must be presented for acceptance before it can be presented for payment : *Express stipulation as to presentment.*

3. In no other case is presentment for acceptance necessary in order to render liable any party to the bill : *No presentment in any other case.*

4. Where the holder of a bill, drawn payable elsewhere than at the place of business or residence of the drawee, has not time, with the exercise of reasonable diligence, to present the bill for acceptance before presenting it for payment on the day that it falls due, the delay caused by presenting the bill for acceptance before presenting it for payment is excused, and does not discharge the drawer and indorsers. *Necessary delay for presentment.*

Time for presenting bill payable after sight. **10.** Subject to the provisions of this Act, when a bill payable after sight is negotiated, the holder must either present it for acceptance or negotiate it within a reasonable time :

If not presented. 2. If he does not do so, the drawer and all indorsers prior to that holder are discharged :

As to reasonable time. 3. In determining what is a reasonable time within the meaning of this section, regard shall be had to the nature of the bill, the usage of trade with respect to similar bills, and the facts of the particular case.

Rules as to presentment for acceptance. **41.** A bill is duly presented for acceptance which is presented in accordance with the following rules :

(*a*) The presentment must be made by or on behalf of the holder to the drawee or to some person authorized to accept or refuse acceptance on his behalf, at a reasonable hour on a business day and before the bill is overdue ;

(*b*) Where a bill is addressed to two or more drawees, who are not partners, presentment must be made to them all, unless one has authority to accept for all, when presentment may be made to him only ;

(*c*) Where the drawee is dead, presentment may be made to his personal representative ;

(*d*) Where authorized by agreement or usage, a presentment through the post office is sufficient :

Excuses for non-presentment. 2. Presentment in accordance with these rules is excused, and a bill may be treated as dishonored by non-acceptance—

(*a*) Where the drawee is dead or bankrupt, or is a fictitious person or a person not having capacity to contract by bill ;

(*b*) Where, after the exercise of reasonable diligence, such presentment cannot be effected ;

(*c*) Where, although the presentment has been irregular, acceptance has been refused on some other ground :

3. The fact that the holder has reason to believe that the bill, on presentment, will be dishonored does not excuse presentment. *When there is no excuse.*

42. When a bill is duly presented for acceptance and is not accepted on the day of presentment or within two days thereafter, the person presenting it must treat it as dishonored by non-acceptance. If he does not, the holder shall lose his right of recourse against the drawer and indorsers. *Non-acceptance.*

43. A bill is dishonored by non-acceptance— *Dishonor by non-acceptance and its consequences.*

(*a*) When it is duly presented for acceptance, and such an acceptance as is prescribed by this Act is refused or cannot be obtained ; or—

(*b*) When presentment for acceptance is excused and the bill is not accepted :

2. Subject to the provisions of this Act, when a bill is dishonored by non-acceptance an immediate right of recourse against the drawer and indorsers accrues to the holder, and no presentment for payment is necessary. *Recourse in such case.*

44. The holder of a bill may refuse to take a qualified acceptance, and if he does not obtain an unqualified acceptance may treat the bill as dishonored by non-acceptance : *As to qualified acceptances.*

2. Where a qualified acceptance is taken, and the drawer or an indorser has not expressly or impliedly authorized the holder to take a qualified acceptance, or does not sub- *If taken without authority.*

sequently assent thereto, such drawer or indorser is discharged from his liability on the bill :

Partial acceptance. The provisions of this sub-section do not apply to a partial acceptance, whereof due notice has been given. Where a foreign bill has been accepted as to part, it must be protested as to the balance :

What shall be deemed assent. 3. When the drawer or indorser of a bill receives notice of a qualified acceptance, and does not within a reasonable time express his dissent to the holder, he shall be deemed to have assented thereto.

Presentment for payment. **45.** Subject to the provisions of this Act, a bill must be duly presented for payment. If it is not so presented, the drawer and indorsers shall be discharged :

Rules as to presentment. 2. A bill is duly presented for payment which is presented in accordance with the following rules :—

(*a*) Where the bill is not payable on demand, presentment must be made on the day it falls due ;

(*b*) Where the bill is payable on demand, then, subject to the provisions of this Act, presentment must be made within a reasonable time after its issue, in order to render the drawer liable, and within a reasonable time after its indorsement, in order to render the indorser liable ;

In determining what is a reasonable time, regard shall be had to the nature of the bill, the usage of trade with regard to similar bills, and the facts of the particular case ;

(*c*) Presentment must be made by the holder or by some person authorized to receive payment on his behalf, at the proper place, as hereinafter defined, either to the person designated by the bill as payer or to his representative or some person authorized to pay or refuse payment on his behalf, if, with the exercise of reasonable diligence, such person can there be found ;

(*d*) A bill is presented at the proper place :—

(1) Where a place of payment is specified, in the bill or acceptance, and the bill is there presented ;

(2) Where no place of payment is specified but the address of the drawee or acceptor is given in the bill, and the bill is there presented ;

(3) Where no place of payment is specified and no address given, and the bill is presented at the drawee's or acceptor's place of business, if known, and if not, at his ordinary residence, if known ;

(4) In any other case, if presented to the drawee or acceptor wherever he can be found, or if presented at his last known place of business or residence :

3. Where a bill is presented at the proper place, and, after the exercise of reasonable diligence, no person authorized to pay or refuse payment can be found there, no further presentment to the drawee or acceptor is required :

4. Where a bill is drawn upon, or accepted by two or more persons who are not partners, and no place of payment is specified, presentment must be made to them all :

5. Where the drawee or acceptor of a bill is dead, and no place of payment is specified, presentment must be made to a personal representative, if such there is, and with the exercise of reasonable diligence he can be found :

6. Where authorized by agreement or usage, a presentment through the post office is sufficient :

7. Where the place of payment specified in the bill or acceptance is any city, town or village, and no place there-

in is specified, and the bill is presented at the drawee's or acceptor's known place of business or known ordinary residence therein, and, if there is no such place of business or residence the bill is presented at the post office, or principal post office in such city, town or village, such presentment is sufficient.

Excuse for delay in presentment for payment. **46.** Delay in making presentment for payment is excused when the delay is caused by circumstances beyond the control of the holder, and not imputable to his default, misconduct or negligence. When the cause of delay ceases to operate, presentment must be made with reasonable diligence :

When such presentment is dispensed with. 2. Presentment for payment is dispensed with —

(a) Where, after the exercise of reasonable diligence, presentment, as required by this Act, cannot be effected;

The fact that the holder has reason to believe that the bill will, on presentment, be dishonored, does not dispense with the necessity for presentment ;

(b) Where the drawee is a fictitious person ;

(c) As regards the drawer, where the drawee or acceptor is not bound, as between himself and the drawer, to accept or pay the bill, and the drawer has no reason to believe that the bill would be paid if presented ;

(d) As regards an indorser, where the bill was accepted or made for the accommodation of that indorser, and he has no reason to expect that the bill would be paid if presented ;

(e) By waiver of presentment, express or implied.

Dishonor by non-payment. **47.** A bill is dishonored by non-payment (a) when it is duly presented for payment and payment is refused or cannot be obtained, or (b) when presentment is excused and the bill is overdue and unpaid :

2. Subject to the provisions of this Act, when a bill is dishonored by non-payment, an immediate right of recourse against the drawer, acceptor and indorsers accrues to the holder.

Recourse in such case.

48. Subject to the provisions of this Act, when a bill has been dishonored by non-acceptance or by non-payment, notice of dishonor must be given to the drawer and each indorser, and any drawer or indorser to whom such notice is not given is discharged ; Provided that—

Notice of dishonor and effect of non-notice.

(a) Where a bill is dishonored by non-acceptance, and notice of dishonor is not given, the rights of a holder in due course subsequent to the omission shall not be prejudiced by the omission ;

(b) Where a bill is dishonored by non-acceptance and due notice of dishonor is given, it shall not be necessary to give notice of a subsequent dishonor by non-payment, unless the bill shall in the meantime have been accepted.

49. Notice of dishonor, in order to be valid and effectual, must be given in accordance with the following rules :—

Rules as to notice of dishonor.

(a) The notice must be given by or on behalf of the holder, or by or on behalf of an indorser who, at the time of giving it, is himself liable on the bill :

(b) Notice of dishonor may be given by an agent either in his own name, or in the name of any party entitled to give notice whether that party is his principal or not ;

(c) Where the notice is given by or on behalf of the holder, it enures for the benefit of all subsequent holders and all prior indorsers who have a right of recourse against the party to whom it is given ;

(*d*) Where notice is given by or on behalf of an indorser entitled to give notice as hereinbefore provided, it enures for the benefit of the holder and all indorsers subsequent to the party to whom notice is given ;

(*e*) The notice may be given in writing or by personal communication, and may be given in any terms which sufficiently identify the bill and intimate that the bill has been dishonored by non-acceptance or non-payment ;

(*f*) The return of a dishonored bill to the drawer or an indorser is, in point of form, deemed a sufficient notice of dishonor ;

(*g*) A written notice need not be signed, and an insufficient written notice may be supplemented and validated by verbal communication. A misdescription of the bill shall not vitiate the notice, unless the party to whom the notice is given is in fact misled thereby ;

(*h*) Where notice of dishonor is required to be given to any person, it may be given either to the party himself, or to his agent in that behalf ;

(*i*) Where the drawer or indorser is dead, and the party giving notice knows it, the notice must be given to a personal representative, if such there is and, with the exercise of reasonable diligence, he can be found ;

(*j*) Where there are two or more drawers and indorsers who are not partners, notice must be given to each of them, unless one of them has authority to receive such notice for the others ;

(*k*) The notice may be given as soon as the bill is dishonored, and must be given not later than the next following juridical or business day :

2. Where a bill, when dishonored, is in the hands of an agent, he may either himself give notice to the parties liable on the bill, or he may give notice to his principal. If he gives notice to his principal, he must do so within the same time as if he were the holder, and the principal, upon receipt of such notice, has himself the same time for giving notice as if the agent had been an independent holder : *If dishonored bill is in hands of an agent.*

3. Where a party to a bill receives due notice of dishonor, he has, after the receipt of such notice, the same period of time for giving notice to antecedent parties that the holder has after the dishonor. *Notice to antecedent parties.*

4. Notice of the protest or dishonor of any bill payable in Canada shall, notwithstanding anything in this section contained, be sufficiently given if it is addressed in due time to any party to such bill entitled to such notice, at his customary address or place of residence or at the place at which such bill is dated, unless any such party has, under his signature, designated another place ; and in such latter case such notice shall be sufficiently given if addressed to him in due time at such other place ; and such notice so addressed shall be sufficient, although the place of residence of such party is other than either of such above-mentioned places ; and such notice shall be deemed to have been duly served and given for all purposes if it is deposited in any post office, with the postage paid thereon, at any time during the day on which such protest or presentment has been made, or on the next following juridical or business day ; such notice shall not be invalid by reason of the fact that the party to whom it is addressed is dead : *When notice shall be given.*

5. Where a notice of dishonor is duly addressed and posted, as above provided, the sender is deemed to have *Miscarriage in post service.*

given due notice of dishonor, notwithstanding any miscarriage by the post office.

Excuses for non notice and delay. **50.** Delay in giving notice of dishonor is excused where the delay is caused by circumstances beyond the control of the party giving notice, and not imputable to his default, misconduct, or negligence: when the cause of delay ceases to operate the notice must be given with reasonable diligence ;

When notice is dispensed with. 2. Notice of dishonor is dispensed with—

(a) When, after the exercise of reasonable diligence, notice as required by this Act cannot be given to or does not reach the drawer or indorser sought to be charged ;

(b) By waiver express or implied : notice of dishonor may be waived before the time of giving notice has arrived, or after the omission to give due notice ;

(c) As regards the drawer, in the following cases, namely, (1) where drawer and drawee are the same person, (2) where the drawee is a fictitious person or a person not having capacity to contract, (3) where the drawer is the person to whom the bill is presented for payment, (4) where the drawee or acceptor is, as between himself and the drawer, under no obligation to accept or pay the bill, (5) where the drawer has countermanded payment ;

(d) As regards the indorser, in the following cases, namely, (1) where the drawee is a fictitious person or a person not having capacity to contract, and the indorser was aware of the fact at the time he indorsed the bill, (2) where the indorser is the person to whom the bill is presented for payment, (3) where the bill was accepted or made for his accommodation.

51. Where an inland bill has been dishonored it may, if the holder thinks fit, be noted and protested for non-acceptance or non-payment, as the case may be ; but, subject to the provisions of this Act with respect to notice of dishonor, it shall not, except in the Province of Quebec, be necessary to note or protest any such bill in order to preserve the recourse against the drawer or indorser ; but in the case of a bill drawn upon any person in the Province of Quebec, or payable or accepted at any place therein, in default of protest for non-acceptance or non-payment, as the case may be, and of notice thereof the parties liable on the bill other than the acceptor are discharged, subject, nevertheless, to the exceptions in this section hereinafter contained.

Noting or protest of bill.

2. Where a foreign bill, appearing on the face of it to be such, has been dishonored by non-acceptance, it must be duly protested for non-acceptance, and where such a bill, which has not been previously dishonored by non-acceptance, is dishonored by non-payment, it must be duly protested for non-payment. If it is not so protested, the drawer and indorsers are discharged. Where a bill does not appear on the face of it to be a foreign bill, protest thereof in case of dishonor, except as in this section provided, is unnecessary :

Protest of foreign bill.

3. A bill which has been protested for non-acceptance, or a bill of which protest for non-acceptance has been waived, may be subsequently protested for non-payment :

Subsequent protest.

4. Subject to the provisions of this Act, when a bill is protested the protest must be made or noted on the day of its dishonor. When a bill has been duly noted, the protest may be subsequently extended as of the date of the noting :

Time for noting.

If acceptor is insolvent.

5. Where the acceptor of a bill becomes bankrupt or suspends payment before it matures, the holder may cause the bill to be protested for better security against the drawer and indorsers :

Where bill must be protested.

6. A bill must be protested at the place where it is dishonored, or at some other place in Canada situate within five miles of the place of presentment and dishonor of such bill : Provided that—

(*a*) When a bill is presented through the post office, and returned by post dishonored, it may be protested at the place to which it is returned, not later than on the day of its return or the next juridical day ;

(*b*) Every protest for dishonor, either for non-acceptance or non-payment, may be made on the day of such dishonor at any time after non-acceptance, or in case of non-payment, at any time after three o'clock in the afternoon :

What protest shall set forth.

7. A protest must contain a copy of the bill, or the original bill may be annexed thereto, and the protest must be signed by the notary making it, and must specify—

(*a*) The person at whose request the bill is protested ;

(*b*) The place and date of protest, the cause or reason for protesting the bill, the demand made, and the answer given, if any, or the fact that the drawee or acceptor could not be found :

If bill is lost, etc.

8. Where a bill is lost or destroyed, or is wrongly or accidentally detained from the person entitled to hold it, or is accidentally retained in a place other than where payable, protest may be made on a copy or written particulars thereof :

Excuses for non-protest and delay.

9. Protest is dispensed with by any circumstances which would dispense with notice of dishonor. Delay in noting

or protesting is excused when the delay is caused by circumstances beyond the control of the holder, and not imputable to his default, misconduct or negligence. When the cause of delay ceases to operate, the bill must be noted or protested with reasonable diligence.

10. No clerk, teller or agent of any bank shall act as a notary in the protesting of any bill or note payable at the bank or at any of the branches of the bank in which he is employed. *Officer of bank not to act as notary.*

52. When no place of payment is specified in the bill or acceptance, presentment for payment is not necessary in order to render the acceptor liable : *Liability of acceptor as to presentment*

2. When a place of payment is specified in the bill or acceptance, the acceptor, in the absence of an express stipulation to that effect, is not discharged by the omission to present the bill for payment on the day that it matures, but if any suit or action be instituted thereon before presentation the costs thereof shall be in tue discretion of the court.

3. In order to render the acceptor of a bill liable, it is not necessary to protest it, or that notice of dishonor should be given to him : *No protest or notice necessary*

4. Where the holder of a bill presents it for payment, he shall exhibit the bill to the person from whom he demands payment, and when a bill is paid the holder shall forthwith deliver it up to the party paying it. *Presentment for payment.*

Liabilities of Parties.

53. A bill, of itself, does not operate as an assignment of funds in the hands of the drawee available for the payment thereof, and the drawee of a bill who does not accept as required by this Act is not liable on the instrument. *Funds in hands of drawer.*

B.E.A. 3

Liability of acceptor.

54. The acceptor of a bill, by accepting it—

(*a*) Engages that he will pay it according to the tenor of his acceptance ;

(*b*) Is precluded from denying to a holder in due course—

(1.) The existence of the drawer, the genuineness of his signature, and his capacity and authority to draw the bill ;

(2.) In the case of a bill payable to drawer's order, the then capacity of the drawer to indorse, but not the genuineness or validity of his indorsement :

(3.) In the case of a bill payable to the order of a third person, the existence of the payee and his then capacity to indorse, but not the genuineness or validity of his indorsement.

Liability of drawer.

55. The drawer of a bill, by drawing it—

(*a*) Engages that on due presentment it shall be accepted and paid according to its tenor, and that if it is dishonored he will compensate the holder or any indorser who is compelled to pay it, provided that the requisite proceedings on dishonor are duly taken ;

(*b*) Is precluded from denying to a holder in due course the existence of the payee and his then capacity to indorse :

Liability of indorser.

2. The indorser of a bill, by indorsing it—

(*a*) Engages that on due presentment it shall be accepted and paid according to its tenor, and that if it is dishonored he will compensate the holder or a subsequent indorser who is compelled to pay it, provided that the requisite proceedings on dishonor are duly taken ;

(*b*) Is precluded from denying to a holder in due course the genuineness and regularity in all respects of the drawer's signature and all previous indorsements ;

(c) Is precluded from denying to his immediate or a subsequent indorsee that the bill was, at the time of his indorsement, a valid and subsisting bill, and that he had then a good title thereto.

56. Where a person signs a bill otherwise than as a drawer or acceptor, he thereby incurs the liabilities of an indorser to a holder in due course, and is subject to all the provisions of this Act respecting indorsers.

Stranger signing bill liable as indorser.

57. Where a bill is dishonored, the measure of damages which shall be deemed to be liquidated damages, shall be as follows:

Measure of damages against parties to dishonored b.

(a) The holder may recover from any party liable on the bill, the drawer who has been compelled to pay the bill may recover from the acceptor, and an indorser who has been compelled to pay the bill may recover from the acceptor or from the drawer, or from a prior indorser—

(1.) The amount of the bill ;

(2.) Interest thereon from the time of presentment for payment, if the bill is payable on demand, and from the maturity of the bill in any other case ;

(3.) The expenses of noting and protest ;

(b) In the case of a bill which has been dishonored abroad, in addition to the above damages, the holder may recover from the drawer or any indorser, and the drawer or an indorser who has been compelled to pay the bill may recover from any party liable to him, the amount of the re-exchange with interest thereon until the time of payment.

58. Where the holder of a bill payable to bearer negotiates it by delivery without indorsing it, he is called a " transferrer by delivery ":

Transferrer by delivery.

Liability   2. A transferrer by delivery is not liable on the instrument :

Warranty.   3. A transferrer by delivery who negotiates a bill thereby warrants to his immediate transferee, being a holder for value, that the bill is what it purports to be, that he has a right to transfer it, and that at the time of transfer he is not aware of any fact which renders it valueless.

Discharge of Bill.

Discharge by payment.   **59**. A bill is discharged by payment in due course by or on behalf of the drawee or acceptor :

Payment in due course.   " Payment in due course " means payment made at or after the maturity of the bill to the holder thereof in good faith and without notice that his title to the bill is defective :

Payment by drawer or indorser, its effect.   2. Subject to the provisions hereinafter contained, when a bill is paid by the drawer or an indorser, it is not discharged ; but—

(*a*) Where a bill payable to, or to the order of, a third party is paid by the drawer, the drawer may enforce payment thereof against the acceptor, but may not re-issue the bill ;

(*b*) Where a bill is paid by an indorser, or where a bill payable to drawer's order is paid by the drawer, the party paying it is remitted to his former rights as regards the acceptor or antecedent parties, and he may, if he thinks fit, strike out his own and subsequent indorsements, and again negotiate the bill :

Accommodation bill.   3. Where an accommodation bill is paid in due course by the party accommodated, the bill is discharged.

60. When the acceptor of a bill is or becomes the holder of it at or after its maturity, in his own right, the bill is discharged.

Acceptor the holder at maturity.

61. When the holder of a bill at or after its maturity absolutely and unconditionally renounces his rights against the acceptor, the bill is discharged: the renunciation must be in writing, unless the bill is delivered up to the acceptor:

Express waiver.

2. The liabilities of any party to a bill may in like manner be renounced by the holder before, at or after its maturity; but nothing in this section shall affect the rights of a holder in due course without notice of renunciation.

The same.

62. Where a bill is intentionally cancelled by the holder or his agent, and the cancellation is apparent thereon, the bill is discharged:

Cancellation of bill.

2. In like manner, any party liable on a bill may be discharged by the intentional cancellation of his signature by the holder or his agent. In such case, any indorser who would have had a right of recourse against the party whose signature is cancelled is also discharged:

Of any signature.

3. A cancellation made unintentionally, or under a mistake, or without the authority of the holder, is inoperative: but where a bill or any signature thereon appears to have been cancelled, the burden of proof lies on the party who alleges that the cancellation was made unintentionally, or under a mistake, or without authority.

Erroneous cancellation.

63. Where a bill or acceptance is materially altered without the assent of all parties liable on the bill, the bill is voided, except as against a party who has himself made,

Alteration of bill.

authorized, or assented to the alteration, and subsequent indorsers :

Proviso. Provided, that where a bill has been materially altered, but the alteration is not apparent, and the bill is in the hands of a holder in due course, such holder may avail himself of the bill as if it had not been altered, and may enforce payment of it according to its original tenor :

What are material alterations. 2. In particular, the following alterations are material, namely, any alteration of the date, the sum payable, the time of payment, the place of payment, and where a bill has been accepted generally, the addition of a place of payment without the acceptor's assent.

Acceptance and Payment for Honor.

Acceptance for honor supra protest. **64.** Where a bill of exchange has been protested for dishonor by non-acceptance, or protested for better security, and is not overdue, any person, not being a party already liable thereon, may, with the consent of the holder, intervene and accept the bill *supra* protest, for the honor of any party liable thereon, or for the honor of the person for whose account the bill is drawn :

In part. 2. A bill may be accepted for honor for part only of the sum for which it is drawn :

Requirements for validity. 3. An acceptance for honor *supra* protest, in order to be valid, must—

(*a*) Be written on the bill, and indicate that it is an acceptance for honor;

(*b*) Be signed by the acceptor for honor :

For whose honor. 4. Where an acceptance for honor does not expressly state for whose honor it is made, it is deemed to be an acceptance for the honor of the drawer :

5. Where a bill payable after sight is accepted for honor, *Computation of time.* its maturity is calculated from the date of protesting for non-acceptance, and not from the date of the acceptance for honor.

65. The acceptor for honor of a bill by accepting it en- *Liability of acceptor for honor.* gages that he will, on due presentment, pay the bill according to the tenor of his acceptance, if it is not paid by the drawee, provided it has been duly presented for payment and protested for non-payment, and that he receives notice of these facts.

2. The acceptor for honor is liable to the holder and to *To what parties.* all parties to the bill subsequent to the party for whose honor he has accepted.

66. Where a dishonored bill has been accepted for honor *Presentment to acceptor for honor.* *supra* protest, or contains a reference in case of need, it must be protested for non-payment before it is presented for payment to the acceptor for honor, or referee in case of need :

2. Where the address of the acceptor for honor is in the *Time for presentment.* same place where the bill is protested for non-payment, the bill must be presented to him not later than the day following its maturity ; and where the address of the acceptor for honor is in some place other than the place where it was protested for non-payment, the bill must be forwarded not later than the day following its maturity for presentment to him :

3. Delay in presentment or non-presentment is excused *Excuses for non-presentment or delay.* by any circumstance which would excuse delay in presentment for payment or non-presentment for payment :

4. When a bill of exchange is dishonored by the acceptor *Protest for non-payment.* for honor, it must be protested for non-payment by him.

Payment for honor *supra* protest. **67.** Where a bill has been protested for non-payment, any person may intervene and pay it *supra* protest for the honor of any party liable thereon, or for the honor of the person for whose account the bill is drawn :

If more than one offer to pay. 2. Where two or more persons offer to pay a bill for the honor of different parties, the person whose payment will discharge most parties to the bill shall have the preference :

Attestation 3. Payment for honor *supra* protest, in order to operate as such and not as a mere voluntary payment, must be attested by a notarial act of honor, which may be appended to the protest or form an extension of it :

Basis thereof. 4. The notarial act of honor must be founded on a declaration made by the payer for honor, or his agent in that behalf, declaring his intention to pay the bill for honor, and for whose honor he pays :

Liabilities and rights in such case. 5. Where a bill has been paid for honor, all parties subsequent to the party for whose honor it is paid are discharged, but the payer for honor is subrogated for and succeeds to both the rights and duties of the holder as regards the party for whose honor he pays, and all parties liable to that party :

Delivery to payer for honor. 6. The payer for honor, on paying to the holder the amount of the bill and the notarial expenses incidental to its dishonor, is entitled to receive both the bill itself and the protest. If the holder does not on demand deliver them up he shall be liable to the payer for honor in damages :

Effect of refusal to receive payment. 7. Where the holder of a bill refuses to receive payment *supra* protest, he shall lose his right of recourse against any party who would have been discharged by such payment.

Lost Instruments.

68. Where a bill has been lost before it is overdue, the person who was holder of it may apply to the drawer to give him another bill of the same tenor, giving security to the drawer, if required, to indemnify him against all persons whatever in case the bill alleged to have been lost shall be found again. *Holder's right to duplicate of lost bill.*

2. If the drawee, on request as aforesaid, refuses to give such duplicate bill, he may be compelled to do so. *If refused.*

69. In any action or proceeding upon a bill, the court or a judge may order that the loss of the instrument shall not be set up, provided an indemnity is given to the satisfaction of the court or judge against the claims of any other person upon the instrument in question. *Action on lost bill.*

Bill in a Set.

70. Where a bill is drawn in a set, each part of the set being numbered, and containing a reference to the other parts, the whole of the parts constitute one bill : *As to bills in sets.*

2. Where the holder of a set indorses two or more parts to different persons, he is liable on every such part, and every indorser subsequent to him is liable on the part he has himself indorsed as if the said parts were separate bills : *If indorsed to different persons.*

3. Where two or more parts of a set are negotiated to different holders in due course, the holder whose title first accrues is, as between such holders, deemed the true owner of the bill ; but nothing in this sub-section shall affect the rights of a person who in due course accepts or pays the part first presented to him : *If negotiated to different holders.*

Acceptance   4. The acceptance may be written on any part, and it must be written on one part only :

If more than one part is accepted.   5. If the drawee accepts more than one part, and such accepted parts get into the hands of different holders in due course, he is liable on every such part as if it were a separate bill :

Payment without delivery of proper part.   6. When the acceptor of a bill drawn in a set pays it without requiring the part bearing his acceptance to be delivered up to him, and that part at maturity is outstanding in the hands of a holder in due course, he is liable to the holder thereof :

Discharge.   7. Subject to the preceding rules, where any one part of a bill drawn in a set is discharged by payment or otherwise, the whole bill is discharged.

Conflict of Laws.

Rules where laws conflict.   **71.** Where a bill drawn in one country is negotiated, accepted or payable in another, the rights, duties and liabilities of the parties thereto are determined as follows :—

Validity, how determined.   (*a*) The validity of a bill as regards requisites in form is determined by the law of the place of issue, and the validity as regards requisites in form of the supervening contracts, such as acceptance, or indorsement, or acceptance *supra* protest, is determined by the law of the place where such contract was made :

Proviso.   Provided that—

(1) Where a bill is issued out of Canada, it is not invalid by reason only that it is not stamped in accordance with the law of the place of issue :

(2) Where a bill, issued out of Canada, conforms, as regards requisites in form, to the law of Canada, it may,

for the purpose of enforcing payment thereof, be treated as valid as between all persons who negotiate, hold or become parties to it in Canada ;

(b) Subject to the provisions of this Act, the interpretation of the drawing, indorsement, acceptance or acceptance *supra* protest of a bill, is determined by the law of the place where such contract is made ;

Drawing indorsement, etc.

Provided, that where an inland bill is indorsed in a foreign country, the indorsement shall, as regards the payer, be interpreted according to the law of Canada ;

Proviso.

(c) The duties of the holder with respect to presentment for acceptance or payment and the necessity for or sufficiency of a protest or notice of dishonor, or otherwise, are determined by the law of the place where the act is done or the bill is dishonored ;

Duties of holder.

(d) Where a bill is drawn out of but payable in Canada, and the sum payable is not expressed in the currency of Canada, the amount shall, in the absence of some express stipulation, be calculated according to the rate of exchange for sight drafts at the place of payment on the day the bill is payable ;

Currency.

(e) Where a bill is drawn in one country and is payable in another, the due date thereof is determined according to the law of the place where it is payable.

Due date.

(f) If a bill or note, presented for acceptance, or payable out of Canada, is protested for non-acceptance or non-payment, a notarial copy of the protest and of the notice of dishonour, and a notarial certificate of the service of such notice, shall be received in all courts, as *prima facie* evidence of such protest, notice and service.

Evidence of protest.

PART III.

CHEQUES ON A BANK.

Cheque defined. **72.** A cheque is a bill of exchange drawn on a bank, payable on demand :

Certain provisions to apply. 2. Except as otherwise provided in this part, the provisions of this Act applicable to a bill of exchange payable on demand apply to a cheque.

Presentment of cheque for payment. **73.** Subject to the provisions of this Act—

(*a*) Where a cheque is not presented for payment within a reasonable time of its issue, and the drawer or the person on whose account it is drawn had the right at the time of such presentment, as between him and the bank, to have the cheque paid, and suffers actual damage through the delay, he is discharged to the extent of such damage, that is to say, to the extent to which such drawer or person is a creditor of such bank to a larger amount than he would have been had such cheque been paid ;

(*b*) In determining what is a reasonable time, regard shall be had to the nature of the instrument, the usage of trade and banks, and the facts of the particular case ;

(*c*) The holder of such cheque, as to which such drawer or person is discharged, shall be a creditor, in lieu of such drawer or person, of such bank to the extent of such discharge, and entitled to recover the amount from it.

Revocation of bank's authority. **74.** The duty and authority of a bank to pay a cheque drawn cn it by its customer are terminated by—

(*a*) Countermand of payment ;

(*b*) Notice of the customer's death.

Crossed Cheques.

75. Where a cheque bears across its face an addition of— General crossing defined.

(*a*) The word "bank" between two parallel transverse lines, either with or without the words " not negotiable ; " or

(*b*) Two parallel transverse lines simply, either with or without the words " not negotiable ; "

That addition constitutes a crossing, and the cheque is crossed generally :

2. Where a cheque bears across its face an addition of Special crossing. the name of a bank, either with or without the words " not negotiable," that addition constitutes a crossing, and the cheque is crossed specially and to that bank.

76. A cheque may be crossed generally or specially by Crossing by drawer or the drawer : after issue.

2. Where a cheque is uncrossed, the holder may cross it General or special. generally or specially :

3. Where a cheque is crossed generally, the holder may May be varied cross it specially :

4. Where a cheque is crossed generally or specially, the Words may be added. holder may add the words " not negotiable ":

5. Where a cheque is crossed specially the bank to which Re-crossing for collec- it is crossed may again cross it specially, to another bank tion. for collection:

6. Where an uncrossed cheque, or a cheque crossed gen- Crossing by bank. erally, is sent to a bank for collection, it may cross it specially to itself :

Uncrossing crossed cheque.

7. A crossed cheque may be reopened or uncrossed by the drawer writing between the transverse lines, and initialling the same, the words " pay cash."

Crossing is a material part of cheque.

77. A crossing authorized by this Act is a material part of the cheque; it shall not be lawful for any person to obliterate or, except as authorized by this Act, to add to or alter the crossing.

78. Where a cheque is crossed specially to more than one bank, except when crossed to another bank as agent for collection, the bank on which it is drawn shall refuse payment thereof:

2. Where the bank on which a cheque so crossed is drawn, nevertheless pays the same, or pays a cheque crossed generally otherwise than to a bank, or, if crossed specially, otherwise than to the bank to which it is crossed, or to the bank acting as its agent for collection, it is liable to the true owner of the cheque for any loss he sustains owing to the cheque having been so paid :

Provided, that where a cheque is presented for payment which does not at the time of presentment appear to be crossed, or to have had a crossing which has been obliterated, or to have been added to or altered otherwise than as authorized by this Act, the bank paying the cheque in good faith and without negligence shall not be responsible or incur any liability, nor shall the payment be questioned by reason of the cheque having been crossed, or of the crossing having been obliterated or having been added to or altered otherwise than as authorized by this Act, and of payment having been made otherwise than to a bank or to the bank to which the cheque is or was crossed, or to the bank acting as its agent for collection, as the case may be.

79. Where the bank, on which a crossed cheque is drawn, in good faith and without negligence pays it, if crossed generally, to a bank, or, if crossed specially, to the bank to which it is crossed, or to a bank acting as its agent for collection, the bank paying the cheque, and if the cheque has come into the hands of the payee, the drawer, shall respectively be entitled to the same rights and be placed in the same position as if payment of the cheque had been made to the true owner thereof. *Protection to bank and drawer where cheque is crossed.*

80. Where a person takes a crossed cheque which bears on it the words "not negotiable," he shall not have and shall not be capable of giving a better title to the cheque than that which had the person from whom he took it. *Effect of crossing on holder.*

81. Where a bank, in good faith and without negligence, receives for a customer payment of a cheque crossed generally or specially to itself, and the customer has no title, or a defective title thereto, the bank shall not incur any liability to the true owner of the cheque by reason only of having received such payment. *Protection to collecting bank.*

PART IV.

PROMISSORY NOTES.

82. A promissory note is an unconditional promise in writing made by one person to another, signed by the maker, engaging to pay, on demand or at a fixed or determinable future time, a sum certain in money, to, or to the order of, a specified person, or to bearer :

2. An instrument in the form of a note payable to maker's order is not a note within the meaning of this section, unless and until it is indorsed by the maker :

3. A note is not invalid by reason only that it contains also a pledge of collateral security with authority to sell or dispose thereof :

4. A note which is, or on the face of it purports to be, both made and payable within Canada, is an inland note : any other note is a foreign note.

83. A promissory note is inchoate and incomplete until delivery thereof to the payee or bearer.

84. A promissory note may be made by two or more makers, and they may be liable thereon jointly, or jointly and severally, according to its tenor :

2. Where a note runs " I promise to pay," and is signed by two or more persons, it is deemed to be their joint and several note.

85. Where a note payable on demand has been indorsed, it must be presented for payment within a reasonable time of the indorsement : if it is not so presented, the indorser is discharged ; if however, with the assent of the indorser it has been delivered as a collateral or continuing security it need not be presented for payment so long as it is held as such security :

2. In determining what is a reasonable time, regard shall be had to the nature of the instrument, the usage of trade, and the facts of the particular case : *Reasonable time.*

3. Where a note payable on demand is negotiated, it is not deemed to be overdue, for the purpose of affecting the holder with defects of title of which he had no notice, by reason that it appears that a reasonable time for presenting it for payment has elapsed since its issue. *Defects without notice.*

86. Where a promissory note is in the body of it made payable at a particular place, it must be presented for payment at that place. But the maker is not discharged by the omission to present the note for payment on the day that it matures. But if any suit or action is instituted thereon against him before presentation, the costs thereof shall be in the discretion of the court. If no place of payment is specified in the body of the note, presentment for payment is not necessary in order to render the maker liable : *Presentment of note for payment.*

2. Presentment for payment is necessary in order to render the indorser of a note liable : *Liability.*

3. Where a note is in the body of it made payable at a particular place, presentment at that place is necessary in order to render an indorser liable; but when a place of payment is indicated by way of memorandum only, presentment at that place is sufficient to render the indorser liable, but a presentment to the maker elsewhere, if sufficient in other respects, shall also suffice. *Place for presentment.*

87. The maker of a promissory note, by making it—

(*a*) Engages that he will pay it according to its tenor ;

(*b*) Is precluded from denying to a holder in due course the existence of the payee and his then capacity to indorse.

Liability of maker.

88. Subject to the provisions in this part, and except as by this section provided, the provisions of this Act relating to bills of exchange apply, with the necessary modifications, to promissory notes :

Application of Part II to notes.

2. In applying those provisions the maker of a note shall be deemed to correspond with the acceptor of a bill, and the first indorser of a note shall be deemed to correspond with the drawer of an accepted bill payable to drawer's order :

Corresponding terms.

3. The following provisions as to bills do not apply to notes, namely, provisions relating to—

What provisions do not apply.

(*a*) Presentment for acceptance ;

(*b*) Acceptance ;

(*c*) Acceptance *supra* protest ;

(*d*) Bills in a set :

4. Where a foreign note is dishonored, protest thereof is unnecessary, except for the preservation of the liabilities of indorsers.

As to foreign note.

PART V.

SUPPLEMENTARY.

89. A thing is deemed to be done in good faith, within _{Good faith} the meaning of this Act, where it is in fact done honestly whether it is done negligently or not.

90. Where, by this Act, any instrument or writing is _{Signature.} required to be signed by any person, it is not necessary that he should sign it with his own hand, but it is sufficient if his signature is written thereon by some other person by or under his authority :

2. In the case of a corporation, where, by this Act, any _{As to corporations.} instrument or writing is required to be signed, it is sufficient if the instrument or writing is duly sealed with the corporate seal; but nothing in this section shall be construed as requiring the bill or note of a corporation to be under seal.

91. Where, by this Act, the time limited for doing any _{Computation of time.} act or thing is less than three days, in reckoning time, non-business days are excluded : "non-business days," for the purposes of this Act, mean the days mentioned in the fourteenth section of this Act ; any other day is a business day.

92. For the purposes of this Act, where a bill or note is _{When noting is equivalent to protest.} required to be protested within a specified time or before some further proceeding is taken, it is sufficient that the bill or note has been noted for protest before the expiration of the specified time or the taking of the proceeding ; and the formal protest may be extended at any time thereafter as of the date of the noting.

Protest when notary is not accessible. **93.** Where a dishonored bill is authorized or required to be protested, and the services of a notary cannot be obtained at the place where the bill is dishonored, any justice of the peace resident in the place may present and protest such bill and give all necessary notices, and shall have all the necessary powers of a notary in respect thereto :

Expenses. 2. The expense of noting and protesting any bill or note, and the postages thereby incurred, shall be allowed and paid to the holder in addition to any interest thereon :

Fees chargeable. 3. Notaries may charge the fees in each Province heretofore allowed them :

Forms. 4. The forms in the first schedule to this Act may be used in noting or protesting any bill or note and in giving notice thereof. A copy of the bill or note and indorsement may be included in the forms, or the original bill or note may be annexed and the necessary changes in that behalf made in the forms :

Evidence of presentation, dishonor and notice. 5. A protest of any bill or note, and any copy thereof as copied by the notary or justice of the peace, shall, in any action be *prima facie* evidence of presentation and dishonor, and also of service of notice of such presentation and dishonor as stated in such protest.

Dividend warrants may be crossed. **94.** The provisions of this Act as to crossed cheques shall apply to a warrant for payment of dividend.

Repeal. **95.** The enactments mentioned in the second schedule to this Act are hereby repealed, as from the commencement of this Act, to the extent in that schedule mentioned :

Provided, that such repeal shall not affect anything done *Proviso.* or suffered, or any right, title or interest acquired or accrued before the commencement of this Act, or any legal proceeding or remedy in respect of any such thing, right, title or interest ;

2. Nothing in this Act or in any repeal effected thereby *"The Bank Act." not affected.* shall affect the provisions of " *The Bank Act :* "

3. The Act of the Parliament of Great Britain, passed *Imperial Acts 15 Geo. III. c. 51 and 17. Geo. III. c. 30 not to apply.* in the fifteenth year of the reign of His late Majesty George III., intituled " An Act to restrain the negotiation of Promissory Notes and Inland Bills of Exchange under a limited sum within that part of Great Britain called England," and the Act of the said Parliament passed in the seventeenth year of His said Majesty's reign, intituled, " An Act for further restraining the negotiation of Promissory Notes and Inland Bills of Exchange under a limited sum within that part of Great Britain called England," shall not extend to or be in force in any Province of Canada, nor shall the said Acts make void any bills, notes, drafts or orders which have been or may be made or uttered therein.

96. Where any Act or document refers to any enact- *Construction with other Acts. etc.* ment repealed by this Act, the Act or document shall be construed and shall operate as if it referred to the corresponding provisions of this Act.

97. This Act shall come into force on the first day of *Commencement of Act.* September next.

SCHEDULE OF FORMS.

FIRST SCHEDULE.

FORM A.

NOTING FOR NON-ACCEPTANCE.

(Copy of Bill and Indorsements.)

On the   18 , the above bill was, by me, at
the request of   , presented for acceptance to
E. F., the drawee, personally (*or*, at his residence, office or
usual place of business), in the city (town *or* village) of
and I received for answer, "   "; The said
bill is therefore noted for non-acceptance.

A. B.,
Notary Public.

(*Date and place.*)   18 .

Due notice of the above was by me served upon {A.B., C.D.,}

the {drawer, indorser,} personally, on the   day of
(*or*, at his residence, office or usual place of business) in
, on the   day of   (*or*, by depositing
such notice, directed to him, at   , in Her Majesty's
post office in the city (town or village), on the   day
of   , and prepaying the postage thereon.)

A. B.,
Notary Public.

(*Date and place.*)   18 .

Form B.

PROTEST FOR NON-ACCEPTANCE OR FOR NON-PAYMENT OF A BILL PAYABLE GENERALLY.

(Copy of Bill and Indorsements.)

On this   day of,   in the year 18   , I, A.B., notary public for the Province of   , dwelling at   , in the Province of   , at the request of   , did exhibit the original bill of exchange, whereof a true copy is above written, unto E.F., the $\left\{\begin{matrix} \text{drawee} \\ \text{acceptor} \end{matrix}\right\}$ thereof personally (*or,* at his residence, office *or* usual place of business) in   , and, speaking to himself (*or* his wife, his clerk, *or* his servant, etc.,) did demand $\left\{\begin{matrix} \text{acceptance} \\ \text{payment} \end{matrix}\right\}$ thereof; unto which demand $\left\{\begin{matrix} \text{he} \\ \text{she} \end{matrix}\right\}$ answered: "   ."

Whereof I, the said notary, at the request aforesaid, have protested, and by these presents do protest against the acceptor, drawer and indorsers (*or* drawer and indorsers) of the said bill, and other parties thereto or therein concerned, for all exchange, re-exchange,, and all costs, damages and interest, present and to come, for want of $\left\{\begin{matrix} \text{acceptance} \\ \text{payment} \end{matrix}\right\}$ of the said bill.

All of which I attest by my signature.
(Protested in duplicate.)

A.B.,
Notary Public.

Form C.

PROTEST FOR NON-ACCEPTANCE OR FOR NON-PAYMENT OF A BILL
PAYABLE AT A STATED PLACE.

(Copy of Bill and Indorsements.)

On this   day of,   , in the year 18 , I,
A.B., notary public for the Province of   , dwelling
at   , in the Province of   , at the request
of   , did exhibit the original bill of exchange,
whereof a true copy is above written, unto E. F., the

$\begin{Bmatrix} \text{drawee} \\ \text{acceptor} \end{Bmatrix}$ thereof, at   , being the stated

place where the said bill is payable, and there, speaking

to   did demand $\begin{Bmatrix} \text{acceptance} \\ \text{payment} \end{Bmatrix}$

of the said bill; unto which demand he answered : "   ."

Whereof I, the said notary, at the request aforesaid, have
protested, and by these presents do protest against the acceptor, drawer and indorsers (or drawer and indorsers) of
the said bill, and all other parties thereto or therein concerned, for all exchange, re-exchange, costs, damages and

interest, present and to come, for want of $\begin{Bmatrix} \text{acceptance} \\ \text{payment} \end{Bmatrix}$

of the said bill.

All of which I attest by my signature.

(Protested in duplicate.)

A.B.,
Notary Public.

Form D.

PROTEST FOR NON-PAYMENT OF A BILL NOTED, BUT NOT PROTESTED, FOR NON-ACCEPTANCE.

If the protest is made by the same notary who noted the bill, it should immediately follow the act of noting and memorandum of service thereof, and begin with the words "and afterwards on, etc.," continuing as in the last preceding form, but introducing between the words "did" and "exhibit," the word "again," and, in a parenthesis, between the words "written" and "unto," the words: "and which bill was by me duly noted for non-acceptance on the , day of ."

But if the protest is not made by the same notary, then it should follow a copy of the original bill and indorsements and noting marked on the bill—and then in the protest introduce, in a parenthesis, between the words "written" and "unto," the words: "and which bill was on the , day of , by , notary public for the Province of , noted for non-acceptance, as appears by his note thereof, marked on the said bill."

Form E.

PROTEST FOR NON-PAYMENT OF A NOTE PAYABLE GENERALLY.

(Copy of Note and Indorsements.)

On this , day of , in the year 18 , I, A.B., notary public for the Province of , dwelling at , in the Province of , at the request of , did exhibit the original promissory note, whereof a true copy is above written, unto , the promisor, personally (or, at his residence, office or usual place of business), in   , and speaking to himself (or his wife, his clerk or his servant. etc.), did demand payment thereof; unto which demand $\begin{Bmatrix} he \\ she \end{Bmatrix}$ answered : "   ."

Wherefore I, the said notary, at the request aforesaid, have protested, and by these presents do protest against the promisor and indorsers of the said note, and all other parties thereto or therein concerned, for all costs, damages and interest, present and to come, for want of payment of the said note.

All of which I attest by my signature.

(Protested in duplicate.)

A.B.,
Notary Public.

Form F.

PROTEST FOR NON-PAYMENT OF A NOTE PAYABLE AT A STATED PLACE.

(Copy of Note and Indorsements.)

On this   day   , in the year 18   , I, A.B., notary public for the Province of   , dwelling at   , in the Province of   , at the request of   , did exhibit the original promissory note, whereof a true copy is above written, unto the promisor, at   , being the stated place where the said note is payable, and there, speaking to did demand payment of the said note, unto which demand he answered : "   ."

Wherefore I, the said notary, at the request aforesaid, have protested, and by these presents do protest against the promisor and indorsers of the said note, and all other parties thereto or therein concerned, for all costs, damages and interest, present and to come, for want of payment of the said note.

All of which I attest by my signature.

(Protested in duplicate.)

A. B.,

Notary Public.

Form G.

NOTARIAL NOTICE OF A NOTING, OR OF A PROTEST FOR NON-ACCEPTANCE, OR OF A PROTEST FOR NON-PAYMENT OF A BILL.

(*Place and date of Noting or of Protest.*)

1st.

To P. Q. (*the drawer.*)

at

Sir,

Your bill of exchange for $, date at the   , upon E. F., in favor of C. D., payable   days after ${\text{sight,} \atop \text{date}}$ was this day, at the request of duly $\begin{Bmatrix} \text{noted} \\ \text{protested} \end{Bmatrix}$ by me for $\begin{Bmatrix} \text{non-acceptance.} \\ \text{non-payment.} \end{Bmatrix}$

A. B.,

Notary Public.

(Place and date of Noting or of Protest.)

2nd.

To C. D. (*indorser*).

(*or* F. G.)

at

Sir,

Mr. P. Q.'s bill of exchange for $, dated at   , the   , upon E. F., in your favor (*or* in favor of C. D.,) payable   days after $\begin{Bmatrix} \text{sight,} \\ \text{date} \end{Bmatrix}$ and by you indorsed, was this day, at the request of   , duly $\begin{Bmatrix} \text{noted} \\ \text{protested} \end{Bmatrix}$ by me for $\begin{Bmatrix} \text{non-acceptance.} \\ \text{non-payment.} \end{Bmatrix}$

A. B.,

Notary Public.

FORM II.

NOTARIAL NOTICE OF PROTEST FOR NON-PAYMENT OF A NOTE.

(Place and date of Protest.)

To   ,

at

Sir,

Mr. P. Q.'s promissory note for $, dated at

, the $\left\{\begin{array}{l}\text{days} \\ \text{months} \\ \text{on ——}\end{array}\right\}$ after date to

$\left\{\begin{array}{l}\text{you} \\ \text{E. F.}\end{array}\right\}$ or order, and indorsed by you, was this day, at the request of   , duly protested by me for non-payment.

A. B.,
Notary Public.

Form I.

NOTARIAL SERVICE OF NOTICE OF A PROTEST FOR NON-ACCEPTANCE
OR NON-PAYMENT OF A BILL, OR OF NON-PAYMENT OF A NOTE
(*to be subjoined to the Protest.*)

And afterwards, I, the aforesaid protesting notary public, did serve due notice, in the form prescribed by law, of the foregoing protest for $\left\{\begin{array}{l}\text{non-acceptance} \\ \text{non-payment}\end{array}\right\}$ of the $\left\{\begin{array}{l}\text{bill} \\ \text{note}\end{array}\right\}$ thereby protested upon $\left\{\begin{array}{l}\text{P. Q.,} \\ \text{C. D.,}\end{array}\right\}$ the $\left\{\begin{array}{l}\text{drawer} \\ \text{indorsers}\end{array}\right\}$ personally, on the   day of (*or*, at his residence, office, or usual place of business) in   , on the day of   ; (*or*, by depositing such notice, directed to the said $\left\{\begin{array}{l}\text{P. Q.,} \\ \text{C. D.,}\end{array}\right\}$ at   in Her Majesty's post office in   on the   day of   , and prepaying the postage thereon.

In testimony whereof, I have, on the last mentioned day and year, at   aforesaid, signed these presents.

A. B.,
Notary Public.

Form J.

PROTEST BY A JUSTICE OF THE PEACE (WHERE THERE IS NO
NOTARY) FOR NON-ACCEPTANCE OF A BILL, OR NON-PAYMENT
OF A BILL OR NOTE.

(Copy of Bill or Note and Indorsement.)

On this   day of   , in the year 18   , I, X. O.,
one of Her Majesty's justices of the peace for the district (*or*
county, etc.), of   in the Province of   , dwelling
at (*or near*) the village of   , in the said district,
there being no practising notary public at or near the said
village (*or any other legal cause*), did, at the request of

and in the presence of

well known unto me, exhibit the

original $\left\{\begin{array}{l}\text{bill}\\\text{note}\end{array}\right\}$ whereof a true copy is above written

unto P. Q., the $\left\{\begin{array}{l}\text{drawer}\\\text{acceptor}\\\text{promissor}\end{array}\right\}$ thereof, personally (*or* at his

residence, office *or* usual place of business) in
and speaking to himself (his wife, his clerk *or* his ser-

vant, etc.), did demand $\left\{\begin{array}{l}\text{acceptance}\\\text{payment}\end{array}\right\}$ thereof, unto which

demand $\left\{\begin{array}{l}\text{he}\\\text{she}\end{array}\right\}$ answered : "   ."

Wherefore I, the said justice of the peace, at the request
aforesaid, have protested, and by these presents do protest

against the $\left\{\begin{array}{l}\text{drawer and indorsers}\\\text{promisor and indorsers}\\\text{acceptor, drawer and indorsers}\end{array}\right\}$ of the said

$\left\{\begin{array}{l}\text{bill}\\\text{note}\end{array}\right\}$ and all other parties thereto and therein concerned, for all exchange, re-exchange, and all costs, damages and interest, present and to come, for want of {acceptance} {payment} of the said {bill.} {note.}

All which is by these presents attested by the signature of the said (*the witness*) and by my hand and seal.

(Protested in duplicate.)

(*Signature of the witness*.)

(*Signature and seal of the J. P.*)

SECOND SCHEDULE.

ENACTMENTS REPEALED.

Province and Chapter.	Title of Act and extent of Repeal.
Dominion of Canada :	
Chap. 123, Revised Statutes.	An Act respecting Bills of Exchange and Promissory Notes. —The whole Act.
Province of Quebec :	
Civil Code of Lower Canada.	Articles 2.279 to 2,354, both inclusive [*].
Nova Scotia :	
Revised Statutes, third series, chap. 82..........	" Of Bills of Exchange and Promissory Notes." Section 2. The other sections of this chapter have been heretofore repealed.
New Brunswick :	
Revised Statutes, chap. 116.	" Of Bills, Notes and Choses in Action." Section 2. The other sections of this chapter have been heretofore repealed.
30 Vic., 1867. chap. 34......	An Act to amend chap. 116 of the Revised Statutes. " Of Bills, Notes and Choses in Action ;" also Act 12th Victoria, chapter 39, relating thereto. Section 1.

* Except in so far as such articles, or any of them, relate to evidence in regard to bills of exchange, cheques and promissory notes.]

INDEX.

B.E.A.   5

ACCEPTANCE— *Continued.*

B E. A.   9

B.E.A. 10